THESEUS
AND THE
MINOTAUR

Could the legend be true?

Pierce Feirtear

OXFORD
UNIVERSITY PRESS

OXFORD
UNIVERSITY PRESS

Great Clarendon Street, Oxford OX2 6DP

Oxford University Press is a department of the University of Oxford.
It furthers the University's objective of excellence in research, scholarship,
and education by publishing worldwide in

Oxford New York

Athens Auckland Bangkok Bogotá Buenos Aires Calcutta
Cape Town Chennai Dar es Salaam Delhi Florence Hong Kong Istanbul
Karachi Kuala Lumpur Madrid Melbourne Mexico City Mumbai
Nairobi Paris São Paulo Shanghai Singapore Taipei Tokyo Toronto Warsaw

with associated companies in Berlin Ibadan

Oxford is a registered trade mark of Oxford University Press
in the UK and in certain other countries

Published in the United Kingdom
by Oxford University Press

Text © Pierce Feirtear 2001

British Library Cataloguing in Publication Data

Data available

ISBN 0 19 917375 3

Available in packs
Ancient Peoples   Pack of Four (one of each book)   ISBN 0 19 917378 8
Ancient Peoples   Class Pack (six of each book)   ISBN 0 19 917379 6

Printed in Hong Kong

Acknowledgements

The Publisher would like to thank the following for permission
to reproduce photographs:

AKG, London: p 31; The Ashmolean Museum, Oxford: pp 5 (left), 12, 13,
14 (middle), 20, 24 (top left & right), 25, 29; Corbis/Rik Ergenbright: p 18;
Corbis/Gail Mooney: p 14 (bottom); Corbis/Gianni Dagli Orti: pp 24 (bottom),
26 (right), 30; Corbis/Vanni Archive: p 22; Corbis/Roger Wood: pp 15, 23 (top);
Magda Hatzopoulos, Greek Embassy, Dublin/Heraklion Branch of the Greek
Women's Lyceum: p 23 (bottom); Scala/Irakleon Museum: p 5 (right).

All other images provided by the author.

Front Cover: Corbis/Gianni Dagli Orti and Corbis/Roger Wood.
Back Cover: Nicki Palin.

Illustrations are by Jeff Anderson, Stefan Chabluk, Antonia Enthoven,
Celia Hart, Chris Molan, Tony Morris, and Thomas Sperling

⧉ CONTENTS

Introduction 4

The legend of Theseus
and the Minotaur 6

Searching for clues 12

The palace at Knossos 14

Who lived at the palace? 16

The labyrinth 18

The Minotaur 22

Theseus 26

Ariadne 28

Conclusion 30

Glossary 32

Index 32

▣ INTRODUCTION

WHAT IS A LEGEND?

A legend is an old story about exciting adventures and heroes. Some legends are hundreds, even thousands, of years old. No one knows who first made them up or wrote them down. Here are examples of some well-known legends:

 *Theseus and the Minotaur*
 *King Arthur and the Knights of the Round Table*
🐂 *The Wooden Horse of Troy.*

Legends can sound historical but they are not actually true. However, let's look at one legend to see if there is any truth in it at all.

The legend of *Theseus and the Minotaur* comes from ancient Greece. It tells how Prince Theseus sailed from Athens to Crete on a daring adventure.

We will also look at the findings of **archaeologists**. These people discover things like jars, coins, or even ruins, that have been buried in the ground since ancient times. Their finds can tell us a lot about life in the past. We will see how well the facts match the legend.

The Legend of Theseus and the Minotaur

Long ago there was a cruel and powerful king called King Minos. He lived in a palace at Knossos on the island of Crete. One day, King Minos asked Daedalus, his master craftsman, to build him a **labyrinth** beneath his palace. Daedalus built one so cunningly that no one who entered it could find their way out again. In the labyrinth, King Minos kept a creature that was half-man, half-bull. It was called the Minotaur and it would attack anyone who came near. Sometimes, King Minos **sacrificed** captives to the Minotaur.

King Minos had a son called Androgeus who was a great athlete. One day, Prince Androgeus sailed away to Greece to take part in the Games at Athens. He won all of the prizes there. The people of Athens were so

furious that an outsider had beaten them that they murdered the prince.

King Minos was very angry. He sailed to Athens with a mighty fleet and attacked the city. He forced the people of Athens, to **surrender**.

Minos wanted to punish the **Athenians** for murdering his son. "Seven boys and seven girls must be sent to my palace every year," he ordered. "There, they will be **sacrificed** to the Minotaur in the **labyrinth**!"

The Athenians had no choice. Fourteen children were chosen. As they were being led down to the waiting ships, a 16-year-old boy stepped forward. His name was Theseus. He was the son of the King of Athens.

"I will take the place of one of the children," he said.

Theseus and the other children were brought before King Minos.

"Tomorrow you will die in the labyrinth," the king said. "But tonight you will be my guests at a feast."

Ariadne, the king's daughter, was at the feast. As soon as she saw Theseus, she fell in love with him.

"I will help you," she whispered and she gave Theseus a ball of golden thread. "Tomorrow, tie this thread to the door of the labyrinth. Let the ball roll and it will lead you to the centre, where the Minotaur hides. Then, you can kill him."

The next day, Theseus did as Ariadne had said. The ball of golden thread ran on and on, leading him down through the **labyrinth**. It became smaller and smaller, and then it stopped. Theseus looked up... and saw the Minotaur!

The monster gave a mighty roar, so loud it shook the walls. Theseus was not afraid. He stepped forward, ready to fight. He and the monster fought long and hard but, in the end, Theseus won. He killed the Minotaur with his bare hands.

When the Minotaur was dead, Theseus and the children followed the golden thread back up through the labyrinth. Ariadne was waiting for them at the door.

"Follow me," she said, "I will guide you to the harbour."

Just as they reached their ship, an alarm was sounded in the palace. When Theseus heard this, he snatched up an oar and smashed holes in the hulls of the other ships. Then he, Ariadne, and the children sailed away from Crete into the night...

▣ SEARCHING FOR CLUES

Could any of this story be true? How can we know what happened so many thousands of years ago? Does any **evidence** remain?

There are some interesting clues. In AD 1900, an **archaeologist** called Arthur Evans discovered the ruins of an ancient palace in Crete. The palace was found in a place that was known to local people as "Knossos".

Aegean Sea

50 kilometres
50 miles

Knossos
Iraklion●□
CRETE

Mediterranean Sea

Arthur Evans, the archaeologist who found the ruins of an ancient palace at Knossos.
▼

We will examine the findings of the archaeologists at Knossos. We will look at:

- the palace
- the people who lived there
- pottery, paintings, and other things found at the site.

Writings from the past may also shed light on the mystery of Knossos.

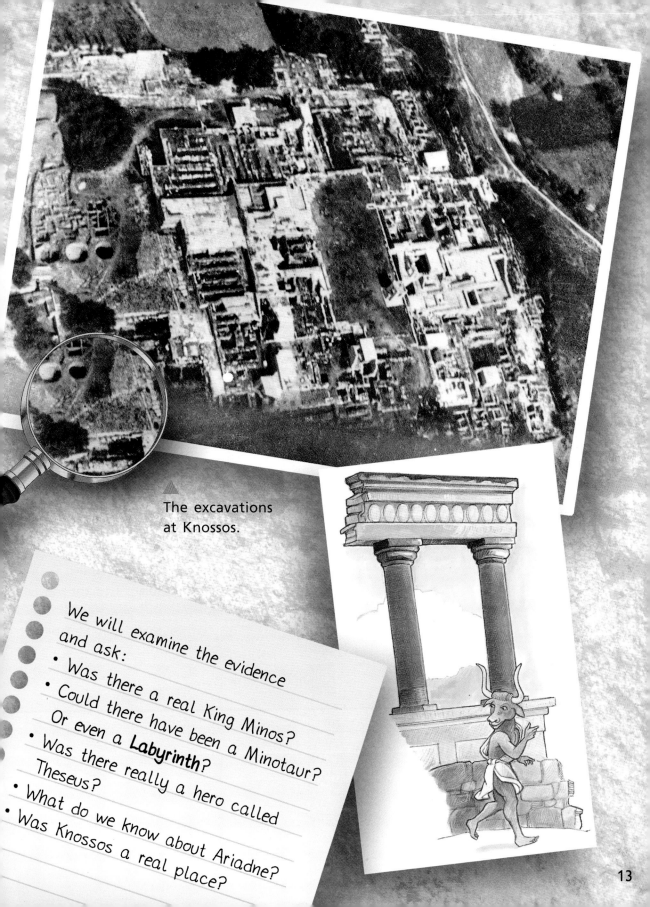

The excavations
at Knossos.

We will examine the evidence
and ask:
- Was there a real King Minos?
- Could there have been a Minotaur?
  Or even a **Labyrinth**?
- Was there really a hero called
  Theseus?
- What do we know about Ariadne?
- Was Knossos a real place?

▣ THE PALACE AT KNOSSOS

At Knossos, **archaeologists** found:

- 🐂 300 rooms
- 🐂 a central court
- 🐂 a throne
- 🐂 huge storage jars.

◀ The ruins covered a huge area.

They worked out that the palace was four storeys high and may have had as many as 1,200 rooms altogether.

The ruins of a city were also found around the palace.

The Throne Room dated from around 1450 BC. The throne is two thousand years older than any other throne in Europe.

▼

Around 3,000 clay **tablets** were also uncovered at the site. The name "Knossos" was written on some of the tablets. This proves that this really was the palace spoken of in the legend.

Dating finds

Pottery

Pottery found at the site can be compared with pieces dated at other historic sites.

Radiocarbon dating

All living things contain **radiocarbon**. When an animal or plant dies, the radiocarbon breaks up at a steady rate. Half of it will disappear over 5,730 years. By measuring the amount of radiocarbon in bones or wood, scientists can work out how old they are.

▲

Some of the pottery at Knossos dated from 2600 BC.

WHO LIVED AT THE PALACE?

Evidence showed that people lived at Knossos from about 3000 BC to 1200 BC.

MINOAN PAINTINGS

These wall paintings of people were found at Knossos. They dated from 1550 BC to 1450 BC and were painted in a free, life-like **style**.

▲ The Dolphin **Fresco**

▲ The Priest-King

▲ The Minoan Ladies

A NEW STYLE

Around 1450 BC, a different painting style appeared. These paintings looked stiff, heavy and formal. The style was the same as that found on mainland Greece. This suggests that in 1450 BC a new ruler came to Knossos from Greece.

▲ These griffins in the Throne Room are painted in the more formal style.

RULER OF THE PALACE

Where there is a palace there is likely to be a ruler. Homer, the Greek poet, was the first to mention King Minos and Knossos. Homer lived in 700 BC, 500 years after the palace was abandoned.

However, there is no mention of King Minos on any of the clay **tablets** found at Knossos.

"Out in the dark blue sea there lies a land called Crete... boasting ninety cities. One of the ninety cities is a great city called Knossos and there King Minos ruled."

THE LABYRINTH

WHAT IS A MAZE?

A maze is a puzzle of many paths that seem to lead in every direction at once. Once inside a maze, it is difficult to know which way to turn, how to find the centre, or how to get out again. It is meant to bewilder and confuse people.

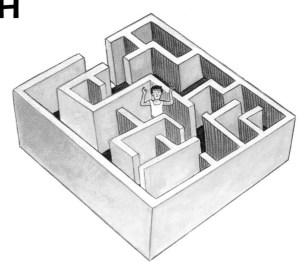

▲ A modern maze

Have you ever been in a maze? If so, was it easy to find your way out of it?

LOOKING FOR THE LABYRINTH

The **legend** says there was a **labyrinth** but is there any evidence of one at Knossos?

 An **aerial view** of the ruins at Knossos.

A **plan** of part of the palace.

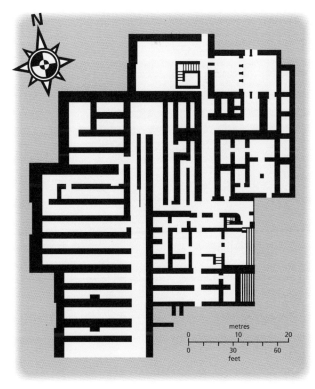

The plan of the palace shows miles of windowless, zig-zagging corridors. Could the palace itself have been thought of as a labyrinth? Most **archaeologists** believe it was not, and that rooms and corridors were simply added to the palace when they were needed.

It is still possible that there was a maze built inside the palace, but that it disappeared over time.

THE DOUBLE AXE

Mysterious carvings of a double axe were found on walls and pillars at Knossos. The Greek word for "double axe" is *labyrs*. Evans saw the link between this word and "labyrinth". So the **labyrinth** could just have been called the "Palace of the Double Axe".

The double axe was an important **symbol** in the palace, so the link between the words "labyrs" and "labyrinth" is strong. Evans's guess is a good one, but it is still a guess.

The word "labyrinthos" has been found on clay **tablets** dug up at Knossos, so it is possible that the people who lived there called the palace by that name.

Long after Knossos had fallen into ruins, a city grew up around it. The people of that city used coins with a simple labyrinth on them. Perhaps this design was inspired by the great maze of ruins outside the city?

Coins from the same city also show the Minotaur...

🔲 THE MINOTAUR

The **legend** says there was a Minotaur, a creature that was half-man, half-bull. Creatures have been found that people did not know existed – dinosaurs, for example. Some creatures, such as the dragon, centaur, or sphinx, live on in stories but have never been seen. There is no evidence to show that a Minotaur existed, but finds at the palace do show that bulls were important.

▼ The Horns of Consecration look like a bull's horns.

BULLS AT KNOSSOS

A huge pair of horns were found on top of the wall at the end of the palace. Many other smaller horns of clay, and small clay statues of bulls were uncovered. Vases and cups decorated with bulls were found too.

The bull, or the horns of the bull, may have been a **symbol** of the power of the king. They may have been used in **ceremonies** at the palace. Someone may have worn a bull costume at these ceremonies. If so, he or she would certainly have looked like a Minotaur…

Perhaps there was a real bull at the palace? Or perhaps a bull-god was worshipped?

◀ Ceremonies are still held at Knossos.

THE BULL-LEAPERS

Paintings of bulls were discovered at Knossos. One of the most interesting is the Bull-Leaping **Fresco**. The painting shows two girls, a boy, and a charging bull. The boy is trying to somersault over the bull's back, while the girl on the right is waiting to catch him.

A copy of the Bull-Leaping Fresco

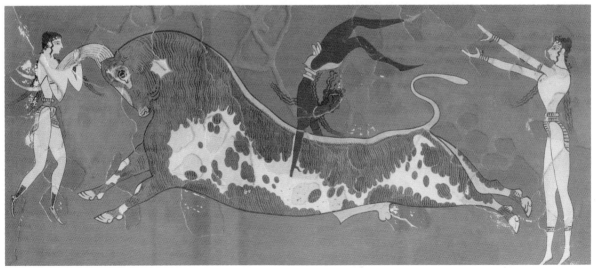

None of the young people have weapons. The bull is not injured in any way. Clearly, this is a very dangerous sport. Anyone trying to do this would probably be hurt or killed.

Who were these bull-leapers? Could they have been the children from Athens who were **sacrificed** to the "bull monster" at Knossos? The question is important, although there is no **evidence** to give an answer.

THE CENTRAL COURT

Could the bull-leaping have taken place in the central court? The pillars of another palace in Crete have grooves where fences may have been put to protect **spectators**. Nothing remains of the pillars that once surrounded the court at Knossos, so we do not know if they had grooves too.

▲ The central court

THESEUS

The **legend** says Theseus came from mainland Greece and killed the Minotaur. Could this have been true?

TWO KINDS OF WRITING

We have already seen that two different painting **styles** were found at the palace. Two different writing styles were found there as well. The first style, called Linear A belonged to Crete. Around 1450 BC, it was replaced by another style, Linear B that came from mainland Greece.

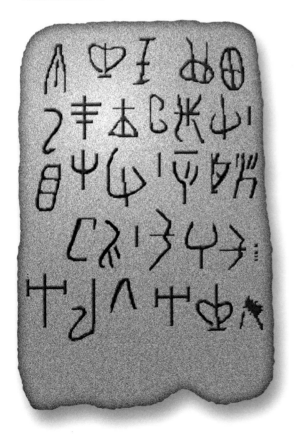

▲ Linear A writing style

▲ Linear B writing style

AN INVADER FROM GREECE

The painting and writing styles changed because the palace rulers changed. An invader had come from mainland Greece. While there is no evidence to suggest that this person was Prince Theseus, it is an exciting possibility.

The legend says that Prince Theseus from mainland Greece killed the Minotaur. The evidence of **archaeology** proves that a Greek invader captured the palace. If we look upon the Minotaur as a **symbol** of the power of the king at Knossos rather than as a real monster, then the legend begins to make sense.

◎ ARIADNE

The name Ariadne means "utterly pure".
It is said that Ariadne was lovely and
dark-haired. As in the case of Prince
Theseus, there is no clear evidence that
a Princess Ariadne existed. However,
her name often comes up in stories
about Knossos.

In his famous poem,
The Iliad, Homer describes:

"...a dancing floor like
the one which Daedalus
drew in the wide spaces
of Knossos for Ariadne
of the lovely hair."

Ariadne gave Theseus a ball of thread, which helped him find his way out of the **labyrinth**. A ball of thread used to be called a "clew". In other words, she gave him a clue!

clue 1 A ball of thread. A thread that guides through a labyrinth. 2 Anything that points to the solution of a mystery.

Archaeologists have uncovered an area at Knossos that was probably used for processions and **ceremonies**. It may also have been used as a floor for dancing. If there was an Ariadne, perhaps she danced here?

CONCLUSION

How much of the **legend** might be true?

The facts are:
- There was a great palace at Knossos.
- Paintings and carvings of bulls were found there.
- The palace was decorated with double axes and *Labyrs* is Greek for "double axe".
- Greeks invaded the palace around 1450 BC.

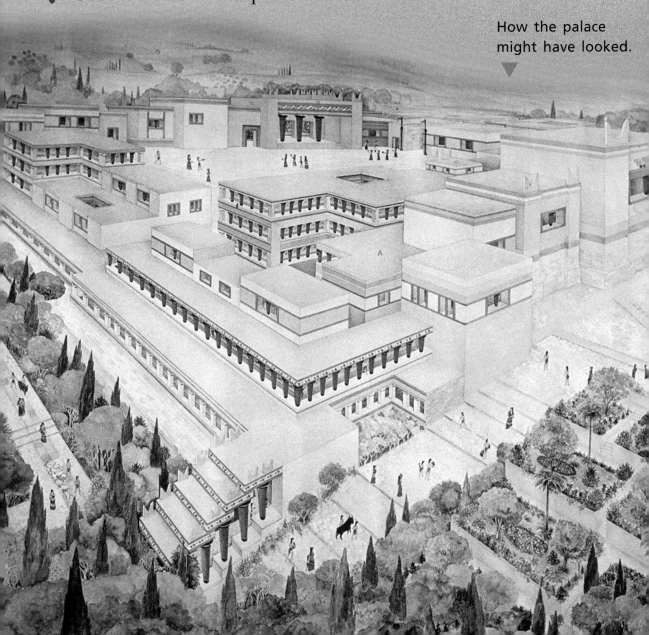

How the palace might have looked.

We cannot prove it, but it seems reasonable to believe that:

🐂 Minos was the King of Knossos.

🐂 The bull was a symbol of his power.

🐂 There was a ceremony involving young people and bulls.

🐂 The word **labyrinth** came from *labyrs,* the Greek for double axe.

🐂 The palace or its ruins seemed like a maze to people who came afterwards.

We do not know if:

🐂 Young people were **sacrificed** to a bull-god.

🐂 Theseus was a real person who invaded Crete.

🐂 Ariadne was a real person who helped Theseus.

🐂 There really was a labyrinth at Knossos.

No one can ever know what really happened in Knossos in 1450 BC. **Archaeology** can only provide clues to the past, but perhaps legends do too?

Arthur Evans with some of the finds from Knossos.

GLOSSARY

aerial view A view from above.
archaeologist A scientist who studies the ancient world.
Athenians People who live in Athens.
ceremony A solemn public event.
evidence The available facts.
fresco A picture that is painted onto fresh, damp plaster on walls.
griffin A creature with an eagle's head and wings, and a lion's body.
labyrinth A very confusing maze.
plan A map, usually of a building.
Radiocarbon A substance found in all living things, or things which were once living.
sacrifice A gift offered to a god.
spectators People who watch a game or ceremony.
style A particular way of doing something.
surrender To give up, and stop fighting.
symbol A sign that stands for something else. A crown is a symbol of royalty.
tablet A block of stone or clay, often with writing carved on it.

INDEX

archaeology 5, 12–15, 19, 27, 31
Ariadne 9–11, 28–29, 31
Arthur Evans 12, 20, 31
Athens 5, 7, 8, 24
central court 14, 25
coins 5, 21
Crete 5, 6, 11, 12, 17, 25, 26, 31
double axe 20, 30
Greece 5, 7, 16–17, 26–27, 30
Homer 17, 28
horns 22–23
King Minos 6–9, 17, 30
Knossos 6, 12–17, 19–21, 24–25, 27–29, 30–31
labyrinth 6, 8–11, 18–21, 29–31
Minotaur 6, 8–11, 21, 22–27
paintings 16–17, 24, 26–27, 30
pottery 5, 14–15, 21–23
radiocarbon dating 15
Theseus 4–5, 8–11, 26–27, 29–31
Throne Room 14, 17
writing 26, 27